AMERICA'S
MOST DIFFICULT
GOLF HOLES

BY

TOM HEPBURN

SELWYN JACOBSON

PRICE/STERN/SLOAN
Publishers, Inc., Los Angeles
1983

PHOTO CREDITS:
Cover and Holes 3 and 18: Australian Pictures, Sydney, Australia
Hole 8: International Press, Auckland, New Zealand
Holes 1, 2, 4-7 and 9-17: Photo Researchers, New York/Bjorn Bolstad, R.G. Everets, Kenneth Fink, Lola Graham, Esther Henderson, Charlie Ott, James R. Simon, Bradley Smith, Arthur Tress

Concept: Tom Hepburn and Selwyn Jacobson
Copyright© 1983 by Tom Hepburn and Selwyn Jacobson
Published by Price/Stern/Sloan Publishers, Inc.
410 North La Cienega Boulevard, Los Angeles, California 90048

ISBN: 0-8431-0916-5
PSS!® is a registered trademark of PRICE/STERN/SLOAN Publishers, Inc.

*P.G.A. Health Warning

Golfing *can* affect your health. If you are thin-skinned, weak-kneed, Lily-livered or suffer from congenital high handicapping, the Publishers and Authors join with the P.G.A. in urging you, before venturing onto any of our illustrated holes, to visit your Professional. And, if you've any sense, your doctor, your ski instructor and the Man from the Prudential.

If you do insist on aiming for the record books (*you qualify just by completing the 18 holes — any score gets a mention*) the following tips may assist you in correct club choice, keeping your score down and getting back alive.

Posthumous Golfers Anonymous

SOME USEFUL DEFINITIONS

The Uphill Lie

McBaffie, in his "*Not On The Level*" (93rd edition) insists the legs be well spread and the club gripped an inch further down the shaft to guarantee accuracy.

Casual Water

Golfers scorn taking the penalty drop from water, when all that's needed is a little application and a firm grip.

The Elements

Inclement weather *never* means an abandoned match. Perhaps an extra sweater, certainly a of Cognac.

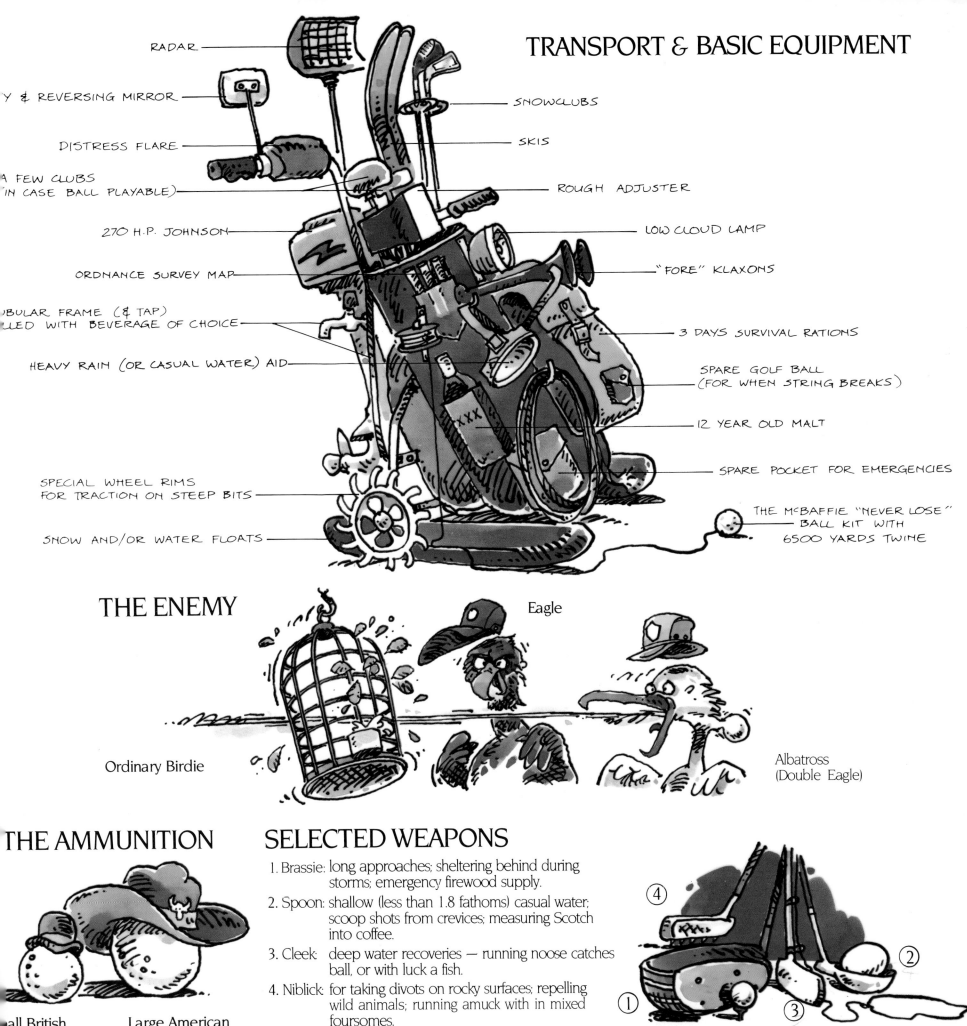

TRANSPORT & BASIC EQUIPMENT

RADAR

Y & REVERSING MIRROR

DISTRESS FLARE

A FEW CLUBS
(IN CASE BALL PLAYABLE)

270 H.P. JOHNSON

ORDNANCE SURVEY MAP

UBULAR FRAME (& TAP)
LLED WITH BEVERAGE OF CHOICE

HEAVY RAIN (OR CASUAL WATER) AID

SPECIAL WHEEL RIMS
FOR TRACTION ON STEEP BITS

SNOW AND/OR WATER FLOATS

SNOWCLUBS

SKIS

ROUGH ADJUSTER

LOW CLOUD LAMP

"FORE" KLAXONS

3 DAYS SURVIVAL RATIONS

SPARE GOLF BALL
(FOR WHEN STRING BREAKS)

12 YEAR OLD MALT

SPARE POCKET FOR EMERGENCIES

THE McBAFFIE "NEVER LOSE"
BALL KIT WITH
6500 YARDS TWINE

THE ENEMY

Ordinary Birdie

Eagle

Albatross
(Double Eagle)

THE AMMUNITION

all British   Large American

SELECTED WEAPONS

1. Brassie: long approaches; sheltering behind during storms; emergency firewood supply.
2. Spoon: shallow (less than 1.8 fathoms) casual water; scoop shots from crevices; measuring Scotch into coffee.
3. Cleek: deep water recoveries — running noose catches ball, or with luck a fish.
4. Niblick: for taking divots on rocky surfaces; repelling wild animals; running amuck with in mixed foursomes.

① ② ③ ④

SWINGERS

450 yards   par 4   1st hole

THIS delightful
golf hole, the first at Canyons, is surely
the finest way to begin a round. Not too
long, an easy par if the ball is struck accurately,
an exhilarating view over the course and an ideal
preparation for the testing long second (par 6),
the tee of which is seen lower right. A certain
lissomeness of limb is advantageous here. But,
thanks to the foresight of Senor Garcia L. de
Cardenas who, in a preliminary survey of the
site for future course layout back in 1540, left
copious notes on locations for swing bridges
and rope ladders, more elderly players can
enjoy a quiet round. The recommended
approach is a full wood to the central plateau,
then a lofted mid-iron *with plenty of spin on the
ball* up to the pin. Take care not to overclub, as
a too-low shot could roll right over the
normally hard-surfaced green, and a valuable
stroke or two would be lost
playing back up.

HEIGH HO, HOPI!

380 yards   par 4   2nd hole

WHEN golfing legends are discussed, as they so often are in the 19th of this, the Valley's most select club, talk invariably turns to Hopalong Hopi, the Hamstrung Caddie, whose instinctive choice of club, tendency to merge into the landscape (often scaring witless ladies pairs on the back 9) and uncanny tracking ability on the longer desert holes has brought many a foursome safely back to the clubhouse with cards intact, if nerves in tatters. It was Hopalong who, singlehanded, ensured that—of the entire field for the '18 Moapa River Open—not one player lost his life over the four days! The nearest thing to a casualty at V.O.F. was at this very hole when Siamese twins Stanislaus and Nikolai O'Keefe, who always played together and indeed were officially counted as one player, disagreed over whose turn it was to putt. Wrestling savagely, they tumbled over the far edge of the green, only to be discovered two days later by Hopalong, unhurt and eager to play on.

MINERVA'S REVENGE

399 yards   par 4   3rd hole

VISITORS to
Yellowstone's demanding course
are (almost) always briefed before teeing
off by a club official, and are careful to avoid the
local hazard which has become internationally
synonymous with trouble — hot water! Less than
accurate drives tend to finish up in one of
Minerva's myriad pools, and if the golfer is not
particularly fast at the start, he may approach his
second only to find the ball rapidly decomposing
in the hot water—out of which, incidentally, he
must play the lie if less than 18 in. deep (local
rule 38f). The Club's membership, never
large and dwindling alarmingly until
Senior Geyserkeeper "Big Bill" Scrotte
introduced judiciously positioned guard
rails, has now stabilized and visitors
are once again welcome to sample
the full 18 holes in comparative
safety.

FALLING ARCHES

360 yards   par 4   4th hole

WITH the best
will in the world our researchers
could not ignore this, the second in our series
from the redoubtable group of tight little courses
scattered over the Arches National Monument's
34,249.94 acres (it was originally thought
that there were 34,250, but allowance had to
be made for an Indian Reservation). In fact it
was Chief Researcher Bledisloe McTuft who was
responsible for the naming of the hole during the
very first round shot at this short but tricky par
4. His congenital foot ailment struck savagely
and suddenly, causing him to drop a good
two inches on the left side half way
through his downswing, top the ball under
the Arch and spoil an otherwise excellent
card. His bellow of combined outrage and agony
was construed by his deafish partner to be "FALLEN
ARCH!" but a passing threesome were to agree
later at the 19th that "fallen," though fairly close,
was not *quite* the word used...

F L O A T E R

490 yards   par 4   5th hole

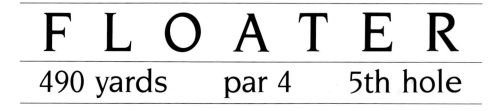

NOT since
the Great Shrinking Tee Disaster
of '88 (which resulted in a contentious
decision by the Match Committee allowing an
ice-pick to be carried as a 15th club) has this hole
been parred. The local rule governing floating
tees clearly states that "…a tee may not be
abandoned until it has shrunk to less than
two square yards in area or the teed ball is
under more than eight inches of water." It was this
rule which nearly caused the downfall of old Otis
Dimwiddle, the Club's Slowest Player, who one
day, intent on his pre-backswing wiggles, failed
to notice that (a) he was standing knee-deep in
water, (b) his ball had floated out of sight
and (c) his three colleagues had selfishly leapt for
safety onto a passing tee. Visitors should remem-
ber that, thanks to the intransigent nature of the
playing surfaces, holes are seldom the same
length two days running. Indeed, they
sometimes disappear from
sight altogether.

EAGLE'S DARE

595 yards (up)   par 5   6th hole

BACK in the
days when golfers were golfers
and women were glad of it, the casual ear
might have picked up a distant high handicapper
singing that old Texas golfing song "...*I'll ride this
course just as long as I please/With a sure-footed
horse between my knees/And I'll score just as long
as they don't plant no trees.../My name is Texas
Dan.*"   The Dan in question is of course the
now legendary Dan McBoone, Scottish
golf pro and gold prospector who, on turning
left instead of carrying straight on to
Sutter's Mill, found himself a little
further south than intended,
and decided he'd walked far enough.
He settled down to design the famous
Big Bend Golf Club's original 18. Our exciting
photograph shows how well Dan used the
natural terrain to make this course
a celebrated feature of the southern circuit.

C A L A M I T Y

630 yards   par 5   7th hole

WHEN Calamity Jane sang so sadly, "*Once I had a secret love/that dwelt within the heart of me…*" she was not, as many people still think today, hankering after her boyfriend in Deadwood City — nor was she, as other, cruel people have suggested, (clearly not Doris Day fans) referring to the lead horse on the Deadwood Stage team — she was in fact thinking back to the halcyon days when her handicap was 4 and dropping and she was twice runner-up in the Badlands G.C.'s Ladies Invitation Silver Cup. Indeed, it was during Jane's third try at this prestigious 36-hole tournament that, reaching the long seventh second time around with a commanding 4-up lead over her nearest rival, Wilhelmina Cody, (+2) she suffered a dizzy spell, mistook her putter for a rattlesnake and, using the quick draw for which she was even then famous, shot her foot off. She never played again, wracked partly by memories of what might have been, partly by her inability to stand up straight.

TOPPERS TERROR

610 yards   par 5   8th hole

JUST before
the halfway mark at this attractive if
straightforward Colorado layout, the first-time
visitor is often surprised when leaving the lush
and verdant fairways of the earlier holes ("...*which
lie deep-meadowed, happy, fair with orchard lawn and
bowery hollows crowned by summer seas*" as Alf
Tennyson so neatly put it the first time he played
the course) for the spartan simplicity of this
intriguing test. Though the route to the green is
clear, the Highest State's higher handicappers
must not fail to take into account the possibility
of extra climbing involved. It was here during the
much talked about Kit Carson Pro-Am second
round in '07 that Ace Carstairs, the Club's wounded
hero (War of '98) duffed his approach from the island fairway
only to realize belatedly he'd forgotten to carry
a spare ball. One tin leg fell off during his hasty
descent. The other quickly jammed in a cleft
and poor Ace was disqualified for
taking more than the allowable five
minutes to play his next shot.

WATER PITY

410 yards   par 4   9th hole

JUDICIOUS
use of natural water is always a
hallmark of competent course architecture,
and here layout expert Jose Mitty, younger
brother of Walt, whose final unsuccessful leap
led to the naming of the falls, not to mention the
building of the bridge, used the natural terrain to
add a dash of piquancy to the hole. On certain
days, spray—and therefore a potentially slippery
club—must be contended with, but the well-
watered green will almost always hold even a
low ball. Jose, who was club captain during
the famous flood of '03, suffered from a
"sympathetic" bladder and seldom made
the swing bridge before succumbing to the
call of the falls. While attempting a spot of mild
relief he was caught unawares by a flash flood
and swept to his doom. The course, though
named in his honor, carries the unusual
spelling above. The Mitty brothers,
though fine golf architects,
were—alas—illiterate.

VIRGIL'S VIGIL

205 yards   par 3   10th hole

The Mt. Whitney course, best known perhaps for its fine views of the Sierra Nevadas, is also (a fact little known outside the Members' Bar) the scene of one of golf's more astonishing feats. During the third round of the Club Championships (Intermediate) in '26, an icy gale blew down off the snows, its attendant drifts playing havoc with the match, and reduced the field to a single foursome. Eventually, after being trapped in a sheltered niche high on the 10th tee for three days and nights with but a marmalade pancake, two green jalapenos and a half bottle of Napa Valley jug red to sustain them, the group decided to play on. Whereupon Virgil G. ("Gassy") Bardahl stepped up to the tee, badly topped a 1-iron and saw his ball slither from icy patch to icy patch, finally lolling into the cup for a hole in one! Alas, only he of his foursome made it back to the clubhouse and the Committee had no recourse but to declare his unsigned card invalid. Ah, the vicissitudes of golf!

THE DRIFTS

500 yards   par 4   11th hole

THE difference
between golfers and players has
seldom been better underlined than in
this photograph. There are some—mere
players all—who dash for the clubhouse at the
first looming of a cloud; others—golfers to a man,
or woman—quietly ignore climatic vagaries and play
steadily on. To such sporting stalwarts a few feet
of snow poses few problems, and when the keenly
awaited new volume from J. Braid Stullwick, "*The
Snow Wedge–Play Winning Shots From Drifts*," is
finally released, snow golfing will undoubtedly
become the "in" thing. One small word of
warning: never shout "Fore!" during
the avalanche season without first glancing carefully
upward. On this very course the late Club
Captain and three colleagues failed to progress
farther that the short 16th ("Precipice")
during that admittedly harsh winter of '93.
Visitors' attention is often drawn to the
discreet plaque at the 19th commemorating
the foursome's untimely disappearance.

BLUE DEEP RICKOFF

290 yards   par 4   12th hole

NEVER a man to mince words, globe-trotting Welsh trick golf exponent Gwilliam Gwilliams, when invited as one of 18 guest golfers to the inaugural hole-naming round at this fine Arizona course, and finding himself obliged to sink a long putt to escape with a two over at this devious par 4, hurled his near-empty bourbon flagon into the crowd, looked back up at the tee, and snarled, "Right bloody prick of a hole this, boyo!" The melodic if slurred lilt in Gwill's voice caused bemused officials, reluctant to admit their ignorance of the Welsh language, to assume he said "Blue Deep Rickoff hole," interpreting the final syllables as Welsh for "double bogey." Students of American golf's colorful history may recall that Gwill never finished that round. Having successfully named his hole, he celebrated by getting well into his second flagon of Old Crow and grappling with his caddie, Miss Millicent Mugabe (no relation); then he collapsed, incoherent but determined, into the big fairway bunker on the long 16th.

JERICHO

190 yards   par 3   13th hole

WHEN pretty Penelope Tree and her old widowed dad Josh first came to California in the late nineties from the Far East (Winchendon, Mass.) it was with a double aim—Penny wanted to be a model and Josh was determined to join a jazz band and get in a bit of golf. That they both succeeded we all now know, but at first, obliged to support poor motherless Penny, Josh had little time away from his work as a Public Convenience inspector in downtown Indio, so he compromised by playing both trumpet and chip shots together. One heady day out in his favorite desert practice patch, Josh hit a pure E above C (the note reputed to have killed Bix Beiderbecke) and simultaneously landed a graceful brassie onto a chosen rock. He was quite startled to find the combination of the sound and the impact of his Dunlop Maxfli DDH 100 Compression against the rocks (shown in our photograph above) caused them to tumble down, domino fashion. Taking this as a sign from Above, Josh devoted the rest of his life to founding the fine Links which today carry his name. The 13th hole, once Josh's practice patch, was named in honor of that notable event.

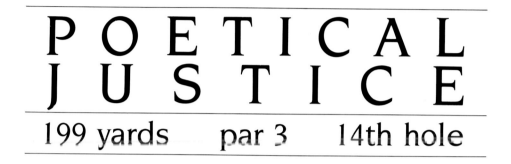

POETICAL JUSTICE

199 yards   par 3   14th hole

THE immortal words of the poet-golfer Robert Burns, so accurately observed in his "Pro's Address to his Caddie" (on losing the Club Championship through Wrong Club Choice at the Eighteenth— *"Wee, sleekit, cow'rin timerous beastie/Oh what a panic's in thy breastie…"*) are more than appropriate at this quaintly different hole. Indeed it was namesake of the poetic genius (and judging from his pursuits while not actually writing poetry, perhaps even a descendant?) Zelda (321 lb) Burns, who added new meaning to that famous poem when she lost her balance attempting an awkward stance for her second, the ball nestling beneath the bench (a Lion's Club donation for senior members). Zelda allowed the panic in her not inconsiderable "breastie" to overcome the advice not to *"start awa sae hastie"* and over she went, clubs and all, to land directly and with, as they say in the C.I.A., extreme prejudice, on an unsuspecting twosome on their way to the next tee. As Robbie Burns wrote so prophetically in his penultimate stanza:
*"The best played shots o' pro's and rabbits gang aft agley
And leave us naught but double bogeys, for promised pars."*

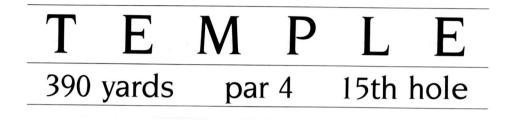

T E M P L E

390 yards   par 4   15th hole

THE sixty million
or so years it took nature to form the
nucleus of what is now the popular group of
three "18's" at Bryce so impressed the inaugural
(1904) Greens Committee that they decided to
do away altogether with boring old fairways and
instead created their golfing paradise around tees
and greens cunningly placed in and about the
spectacular rock formations. True, this can cause
the odd problem, as evidenced in our photograph
of the 15th, a hole needing at any time extra
care over club choice. Here a visitor has driven
too low, only to see his ball rebound viciously off
the rock face, narrowly miss his partner (seen
ducking precariously close to the edge) and
disappear down into the valley below. And
the following hole, the 16th—the tee is
just below the access bridge—is an
even trickier proposition, its green
both hidden and elevated behind
the white marker post, a testing
750 yards distant.

THE SPLITS

505 yards   par 4   16th hole

IT takes a
big hitter to try the direct line here,
and for most the decision is into
which crevice or snowdrift to drop a ball
to avoid that frustrating roll back down. And
pity the putt which, "given a look at it," trickles
over the lip of the green and plummets the
4800 feet to the valley below! But was this hole
always so difficult? The Oldest Member has been
known, while in his cups, to mutter darkly of long
ago, when the green rested atop a full Dome,
and of the legendary Slicin' Sammy Shane,
Hardest Hitter in the West. Seems Sam went for
the big one here at the 16th, hit too low and
cracked his ball against a weak spot on the
Dome, half of which sheared off and fell
away. At this point the Oldest Member
usually becomes incoherent and no
matter how many drinks are applied,
refuses to say which type of
ball Sammy used.

D O U B L E
T R O U B L E

260 yards   par 3   17th hole

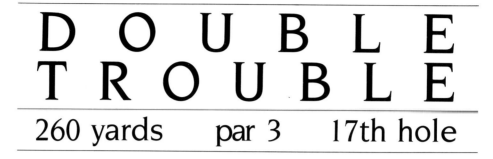

"**A**S the grains
of sand are in the desert, so are the rotten
lies awaiting the unwary on the Arches' course." These
propitious words were first spoken by visiting Mexican
amateur and part-time hat dancer Ludovic Gonzales
during his fateful after-dinner speech on coming
last in the monthly longest wedge competition.
Our photograph suggests why Ludo felt
the way he did—decisions, decisions! To go
under the arch with a long iron and risk a
bounce back, or to gamble a lofted 5-wood
over the top and perhaps have to play a
second off the ledge? The keen eye will
spot the ball from just such a shot
flying up towards the pair waiting on
top, but the trajectory must be
absolutely accurate or the
possibility of a double bogey
(or worse) looms.

HEAD HEIGHTS

290 yards   par 3   18th hole

NEVER
an easy hole to par,
this exciting challenge on
Rushmore's lesser known "East 18"
first came into prominence back in '27
when four keen amateurs, George, Tom, Abe
and Ted (at that time mere weekday members)
each holed out in one during the same round *and
with the same mashie-niblick*! So impressed was the
Match Committee with this sterling achievement
that they commissioned busts of the famous
foursome for the President's Bar mantelshelf
at the 19th. Unfortunately Arbuthnot Mulliner,
the club's sculptor, though playing off a six,
was also a bit deaf and misunderstood his
instructions. Thus instead of four golfers
immortalized in the President's Bar, four
Presidents began to appear on the
1st hole—since 1941 a star
attraction on the
U.S.A. circuit.

PRICE/STERN/SLOAN *Publishers, Inc.*
410 North La Cienega Boulevard, Los Angeles, California 90048